24

24 Hours in the Day

DAVID GILNA

978-1-915502-91-9 © David Gilna 2024

All rights reserved. No part of this book may be reproduced, stored in a retrieval system, or transmitted by any means, electronic, mechanical, photocopying, recording or otherwise without written permission from the author. Published in Ireland by Orla Kelly Publishing.

Orla Kelly Publishing
27 Kilbrody,
Mount Oval,
Rochestown,
Cork,
Ireland.

Dedication

Thanks a thousand to my parents, Pat and Bernadette Gilna, who encouraged me to chase my dreams. To my sister and brother, Jenny and Brian, my nieces Rebecca, Amy, Megan, and Nicole, and my nephews Nathan, Max, Christopher, thank you for your unwavering support.

To all my friends and family, my inner circle, and the community of Swords, Co Dublin, your encouragement has been invaluable. Special thanks to Louise Anderson, Orla Kelly Publishing, Photographer Phil Traynor, and my writing collaborators Frank Allen, Orla Doherty, John McDonagh, and Elaine Murphy.

To Charles O'Brien, Co-Founder of Theatre Under The Big Top, Sinéad Kavanagh, The 1916 Centenary Performing Arts Club, Origin Theatre, Mick Mellamphy, Catherine Murnin, and We Are Global Irish.

To everyone who has supported my creative ventures over the past twenty-four years, I'm forever grateful. To my mentors who inspired me to never stop creating. To my family and friends I've lost along the way, your spirits continue to inspire me.

Onwards.

David

About the Author

David Gilna is an award-winning Irish playwright, actor, and screenwriter hailing from Swords, Co Dublin. With an international stage career that spans continents, David has enthralled audiences as both an actor and playwright, bringing powerful stories to life. As a filmmaker, his award-winning work has garnered acclaim and showcased his unparalleled talent for storytelling.

Deeply proud of his roots and local community, David finds inspiration in his hometown of North County Dublin. He enjoys the banter and conversation found over pints of stout and whiskey chasers in his local pub, where many a story has been both shared and born.

While best known for his artistic achievements, a peculiar twist in David's life is his experience of being struck by lightning—an event he chooses never to talk about! Thanks a thousand to those who have supported his creative ventures and everyone who has bought this book and supported David's journey.

Connect with David Gilna on social media to follow his latest projects and adventures.

Contents

Dedication iii
About the Author iv
1 1
2 2
3 4
4 5
5 6
6 8
7 10
8 12
9 14
10 15
11 16
12 17
13 18
14 20
15 21
16 22
17 24
18 25
19 26
20 28
21 29
22 30
23 32
24 34
About the Publisher 35
Please Spread the Word 36

1

Drown out the noise,
And heal your pain.
A mirage of marching glowing lanterns,
Will fight those demons and shadows away.

Close your eyes,
Flick the switch to ignite your killer blow.
For you have all the answers,
Just the wrong people tried to hush your inner glow.

When you feel that flow,
You ride the whistling heavens of evanescence.
For you are free from the doubters,
Your smile lights the way gladly.

I want you to remember,
That you make the world a better place.
When you believe in the magic that is you,
A beacon of light shines through.

Open your eyes,
And believe in you like I do.
Forever dancing & romancing,
In a field of dreams that we created,
In awe of your inner glow.

2

As this Autumn day gently falls,
My body disconnects from the world outside.
Me heart recalls a time that tore my soul,
Mind heals, yet scars dwell deep within my tapestry.

An anniversary nears, a date we cherish in pain.
Mind dances among stars of a once joyous romance.
Unexpected grief takes its time, me friend,
A farewell, whispered for the very last time.

I find solace in nature,
Walks by the ocean, along the banks of rivers, lighten me load.
Whistling leaves, a reminder of peace and playfulness,
I'm a spiritual auld soul, sensing angels and guiding energy waves.

I bleed emotions onto these pages,
For we are a tribe, bearing the weight of goodbyes,
To mothers, fathers, brothers, sisters, sons, daughters, and friends,
No chance for one last exchange of love's words.

But as time moves, as life dances on,
I remember your voice, our laughter around me kitchen table.
This poem doesn't seek sorrow;
It's a reminder that it's okay to feel lost or burn with rage.

For this is life, navigating the path of grief.
Tonight, I'll raise a pint of stout with a whiskey chaser,
To you, my dear comrade, me friend,
Knowing you guide my steps through the darkest of times.

Tonight, I celebrate your life,
The joys, the madness, the best of times,
The memories etched into my heart,
In this life and the next.

Forever a storyteller with a penchant for spirits,
Kindling candles to radiate hope,
To all me brothers and sisters,
As this Autumn day bids us farewell.

3

Close your eyes, recall those by your side,
Friends, not by birth but life's turning tide.
In this journey, souls may intertwine,
Through shadows and laughter, the bond will shine.

A friend speaks truth, stands in your defence,
Through odds and flaws, in every consequence.
We all change, evolving as we roam,
Yet cherish the shared laughter, where hearts find home.

Celebrate the colours that friendships lend,
Complications may rise, life may rend.
In this fleeting time, life's brief trend,
Friends illuminate the dark, a bond to mend.

Family may weave complexity's thread,
Life's cruelty may bear a weighty tread.
Yet, in this short span we call our own,
A friend, a guide, a beacon brightly shown.

At your lowest, they're present, steadfast and true,
A light in the dark, to help you renew.
This drunken playwright, with words uncoiled,
Urges you to acknowledge a friendship, loyal.

Guiding bonds, whether in the sky,
Or a local park as the pub hours fly.
To kinship, to honesty, and truth untold,
Sláinte to the friendships that never grow old.

4

A calling whispers to the heart, not driven by the gold,
In realms of creativity, where wondrous tales are told.
Slightly eccentric, a touch of the divine,
A passion that's your calling card, a treasure you enshrine.

To weave stories with heart and soul, to touch a living crowd,
Or stir the depths of human hearts, express emotions loud.
In highs that touch the heavens, or chats with an auld dear,
Private tales, public delights, moments held so dear.

Yet, pitfalls lie along the path, a hand stretched out in need,
A begging bowl to giants, where the funding lines are freed.
In silence, let no shadows in, extinguish your soul's flame,
Embrace the chosen path, cherish each creative claim.

Magic sparks on stage or screen, etched in memory's grace,
The life of an artist, a journey to embrace.
True to your creative soul, reflecting as you go,
Undervalue not your talents, let your creative river flow.

In moments of solace, when the towel feels near,
Remember the power of the blank page, the audience's cheer.
An engagement, an electric high, words can't quite express,
A proud Irish playwright from North County Dublin, tales to confess.

Blessed to keep on creating, in darkness and in light,
Through devilment and company, the storyteller's delight.
Dance into the night, free from constraints that bind,
Fuel the creative spark, the strength within your mind.

5

Today dawned with a smile upon me face,
For a decade, I wandered as the man in black,
Sharing only what I chose with the world,
Yet harbouring within an icy wall of defence.

Comfortable in me solitary skin,
A forever drinker and bachelor with writing problems,
A life I owned and embraced sans regrets,
Walking the line solo, with confidence unbridled.

Until one day, your gaze, so full of love,
Caught me roving eye with a cheeky wink,
A spark of conversation ignited,
The songbirds gathered around us that night,
For we always knew that spark was there,
Though our paths had led us to foreign seas and adventures.

On that night, our lips met, melting the ice,
Unease gripped me, every instinct urged flight,
Yet, you opened a dormant portal,
A spark, a chemistry, undeniable.

Every glance across a crowded room,
Brought joy to me life, eyes fixed only on you.
Two lovers, no false promises,
No lies about a future or empty plans,
Living only in the moment.

Over time, a transformation began,
Lying by your side, stars smiling above,
A fire ignited in me once-foolish heart,
From a man who claimed he'd find solace in solitude.

In the words of the greats, you're a rare thing,
I'd fallen in love with you,
Perhaps, whiskey-fuelled confessions escaped me lips,
But you implored me to remember what I drunkenly said in a night of passion,
And today, I do,
I love you.

So, this is a poem for you,
Lost in your loving eyes for days on end,
Boldly kissing you in public, who the feck is this?
A man forever in black, cheeky and devilish,
In love with your stunning beauty, wit, and strength of steel.

Today, I smile, no need to run away,
Today, you're me girlfriend, and we promise only what we can,
Forever entwined in our days, Heart and soul, yours to hold.

Now, pour me a drink, a double whiskey, please,
A gin and soda for you,
Now the world shall know,
I love you.

6

In the realm of stage, he cast his grand presence,
Conal Kearney, the maestro of stage essence.
The final curtain falls, a bow to the great,
A mentor, a coach, unlocking fate.

A call from Jill Doyle, a twist of destiny's hand,
Led me to a coach who'd help me understand.
At times, a chair toss seemed the perfect play,
Yet you pushed me forward, guiding the way.

From the Abbey's stages in '74 to '91,
A thespian journey, decades of fun.
Our paths crossed at The Factory's embrace,
Growing from there, to London's bright space.

For a West End role, you sculpted me skill,
Goals achieved, yet you craved for more thrill.
Our clashes, a testament to wild, stubborn heart,
Your voice echoing, a stage-master's art.

In language and diction, your command stood tall,
The grandson of Peader Kearney, we heed the call.
As you directed me work, a proud Irish flame,
Waterloo's stages etched with our shared name.

Tennessee Williams, Keats, and Cohen's grace,
In the rehearsal room, a sacred space.
An education profound, a legacy so bright,
Conal Kearney, an acting giant's light.

With history woven in the fabric of me play,
Opportunities that shaped life's course in every way.
A proud former student, your wisdom rings true,
For in your footsteps, greatness I pursue.

In the words you favoured, a poetic adieu,
"The world is lit by lightning!" Now, candles we strew.
Blow them out, dear Conal, a final goodbye,
In the realm of stage, your spirit will fly.

7

On January's fifteenth night, a tale began to unfold,
In the city that never sleeps, a story to be told.
A Bolt From D'Blue took the stage, at The New York Irish Center,
As part of 1st Irish Festival, a moment to remember.

In minus fifteen chills, inside the theatre's embrace,
Magic brewed within, filling the sacred space.
Following heroes, Behan and Wilde's illustrious trace,
I danced on boards where legends once found grace.

A brotherhood with Mick Mellamphy, a cowboy true,
Supporting each other, opportunities grew.
He stepped into The O'Rahilly's role, a story to construe,
Touring America, tales of heroes from The 1916 Easter Rising we strew.

New York City, a beacon for this Irish playwright's flight,
Everything flourished, career taking new height.
Sold-out audiences, applause echoing through the night,
The land of dreams and opportunities, shining so bright.

The Lower East Side called, a New York tale begun,
A home found, with bandits and republicans, under La Vie Bohème's sun.
As career blossomed, love's embrace begun,
A lady, a muse, igniting the soul, forever wanting more, all in one.

Today marks the start of ventures anew,
Following hearts, on an adventure to pursue.
To the venues, the reviewers, and companies who gave a spotlight true,
A thousand thanks, a heartfelt salute to you.

To new friends who showed the New York session,
Lock-ins and traditions, a city in full expression.
To dreamers landing, embracing glorious confession,
Into this merry dance, a delightful possession.

Now into me fourth 1st Irish Festival, a tale to renew,
Announcements, shows, screenplays, a creative brew.
A Bolt From D'Blue, Nancy & Michael & The Bronx Gamble too,
Found a home in this city, where dreams come true.

A thank you for two years of incredible ride,
Touring America's landscapes, finding a new stride.
A community, a home, a place to showcase pride,
This is just the beginning, with more to confide.

8

In the eyes of me reflection, I see a land so green,
A history of struggle, where freedom was a dream.
Eight centuries of oppression, a tale so long,
Irish hearts beat strong, singing a freedom song.

Wolfe Tone's whispers echo in the Irish breeze,
A call for united hearts, breaking shackles with ease.
Robert Emmet's flame, burning bright and true,
In the fight for liberty, a sacrifice we knew.

Michael Collins, strategist in the shadows cast,
Navigating treacherous paths, for a freedom that would last.
James Connolly's spirit, a rebel's fervent creed,
A vision of justice, for every Irish seed.

The O'Rahilly faced bullets, a hero in the street,
As 1916's children danced to a revolutionary beat.
Men, women, and children, side by side,
In the quest for a nation, in Easter's rising tide.

Through valleys of hardship, a united stand,
For Ireland's democracy, they took a courageous stand.
Their shadows linger, whispering in the Irish air,
A dream of unity, a nation free and fair.

As a son of North County Dublin, I reflect,
On the heroes and heroines, courage they inject.
In the echoes of their struggles, I find my voice,
A proud Irish playwright, embracing their choice.

The dream of a united land, my hope endures,
Through the poetry of freedom, Ireland matures.
In the eyes of my reflection, I see a nation's plea,
For a future united, where all of Ireland is free.

9

In vibrant Amsterdam, we took a flight,
Two souls lost in the canals, oh, what a sight.
Mushroom tea sparked talks with Van Gogh's grace,
Baroque to Gothic, the Rijks museum we embrace.

Above, smoke clouds danced, a laughter symphony,
Holding hands, lost in the city's vibrant cacophony.
Amsterdam's Sex Museum shared tales untold,
Bicycle lanes and tulips, a story to be scrolled.

Through Amsterdam Zoo, butterflies in our stride,
On the 17th floor, love in bubbles did reside.
Sunset hues painted a canvas above,
Lost in each other, in the city of love.

Amsterdam's music, a time-traveling spell,
Our brains reset, and our bodies swell.
In this beautiful city, where dreams unfurl,
Two souls, lost in love's whirl.

10

In the dance of love, you led the way,
A beacon of strength, lighting our day.
A majestic magician, pain you'd conceal,
Challenging my wrongs with a look that could heal.

Your eyes spoke volumes, a thousand words deep,
Sinking ships or guiding lost sheep.
A life-giver, my Mother, a Warrior so bold,
Forged in spirituality, her story unfolds.

No apologies for who she became,
A Lady through and through, not seeking fame.
Dancing angels, second chances, her creed,
A soul unburdened, in laughter she'd feed.

Her love infectious, her laughter a song,
A life-giver, my Mother, where she belongs.
In warm embraces, grandchildren find delight,
Thanks a thousand for your love, shining bright.

As your light dims on this planet we roam,
Your soul's dance forever our eternal home.
Embracing shadows, unafraid of the afterlife,
An Earth Angel who graced us with endless life.

Today, a celebration of women so divine,
Dancing, loving, laughing in life's grand design.
Happy Mother's Day to every life-giving spark,
To the women who shaped us, lighting the dark.

11

Today we celebrate a special birth,
Seventy-five years, a life of worth.
Patrick Gilna, father and a friend,
Family first, a love that'll never end.

In the community, his spirit soars,
An open door, advice he pours.
Around the table, whiskey in hand,
Politics, business, his wisdom grand.

A proud Irishman, a challenge he'll throw,
Knowledge and questions in a steady flow.
A man of music, infectious delight,
Inspiring my journey, taking flight.

Children, grandchildren, all adore,
His wife of fifty years, smiling evermore.
Patrick, Pat, but never Paddy,
A true Irishman, spirit never shoddy.
Bleeding green, a West Brit he'll disdain,

Manchester United, Shamrock Rovers, his soccer reign.
By the TV's bright glow, a glass in hand,
Honouring Patrick Gilna, a life so grand.
Happy 75th Birthday, inspiring still,
A legacy of love, an eternal thrill.

12

I hope you don't reach this chapter in life,
Trapped in the waiting room of fate's unknown strife.
Grim shadows lingering, a spectre of doubt,
A test of faith as you navigate this route.

But look at your life as a series of chapters,
Embrace the moments that sparked love and captured
The essence of adventure, vivid and true,
For in those memories, hope finds its hue.

No matter the outcome, don't let it dictate
The focus of life, or the joy you create.
Sit in the waiting room with a mindful breath,
Reflect on the beauty that surrounds, even in death.

Today is a celebration, a testament to the past,
Bless the journey that brought you here at last.
Remember to breathe, let hope be your guide,
For in this waiting room, strength resides.

13

In the heart of the big top, where dreams take flight,
Herta Fossett, a Queen of Circus, graced the night.
Under the canvas sky, a magic world unveiled,
Her wagon held stories, like secrets never curtailed.

Charles O'Brien, extended his hand,
Inviting me to join this enchanted land.
The Theatre Under The Big Top, a stage so grand,
From 2008 to 2020, where memories would stand.

Electric Picnic, a festival ablaze,
With plays and performances, met with amaze.
Fossett's Circus, the heart and soul,
Herta's wagon, where stories would unroll.

Amidst the swirl of smoke and the circus haze,
Tea, coffee, and cakes, in the warmth of her gaze.
Dogs by her side, family all around,
In the circle of magic, advice profound.
On the road, still touring, Herta took her final bow,
A Queen on wheels, as she does now.
The Festival Nanny, a regal stroll,
Through Electric Picnic, a grand patrol.

Early Sunday bands, with Herta in tow,
A journey through the festival's lively flow.
Not just a spectator, not just a fan,
But a Queen on wheels, meeting each woman and man.

In Swords, County Dublin, and far beyond,
Every arrival, a spectacle fond.
The world of showbiz, in her eyes gleamed,
A woman of courage, the circus dreamed.

Her death notice, a sombre tone,
A life dedicated, a love deeply known.
With Teddy by her side, they built a legacy,
Devoted to Fossett's Circus, their eternal elegy.

A mother, a grandmother, a guiding light,
In Fossett's Circus, she shone so bright.
A loss profound, felt across the land,
Herta, forever in the circus sand.

As the canvas falls, and the lights dim low,
A farewell to the Queen, a bittersweet blow.
To Herta Fossett, on the circus stage,
A final bow, an eternal engage.

Her spirit lives on in the circus air,
In stories told, in memories rare.
May the big top echo her laughter and glee,
A tribute to Herta, the Queen of Circus, eternally.

14

In silence, my heart ceased its rhythmic beat,
News of your departure, a tragic, crushing feat.
Grey shadows draped over plans we had spun,
Vaporized dreams, a life undone.

Grief, a relentless tide, in waves it came,
Loss of someone cherished, life is not the same.
In unannounced moments, the news unfurls,
Candles flicker, their glow, my healing pearls.

Yet, in the quiet, a connection lingers,
Your laughter echoes, around my kitchen singers.
Your voice may fade, but your spirit persists,
A subtle presence in the moments I've missed.

Tears of pain, tonight, my eyes may shed,
Yet within, a smile, for the life we led.
Blessed to know you, wit and charm combined,
A radiant presence, forever enshrined.

Alone at the bar, a solitary toast,
Your presence, an everlasting, warming ghost.
Rest in peace, dear one, in eternity's scope,
Tomorrow dawns, carrying the torch of hope.

15

In Swords, where the Jacko winds its course,
Banter flows with community force.
Round tower stands tall, Swords Castle in thrall,
Where names are known, and tales take their course!

In Swords, where wit and charm entwine,
Pubs buzzing with banter, warmth divine.
Up D'Parish, where names are known,
The heart of the community, seeds of love are sown.

16

At 92, the legendary Malachy McCourt has left us,
A gifted actor, writer, raconteur, and storyteller, the finest.
Over the past two years, I've had three plays staged in New York's embrace,
I found a friend in Malachy, an Irish icon of grace.

His support unwavering, his radio show a platform grand,
On WBAI Radio, our talks with McDonagh about arts and history were carefully planned.
Praising my work, he compared me to Behan and Wilde, my heroes bold,
He opened doors, shared mischievous adventures, stories untold.

A deal we struck, an honour bestowed, a pact so dear,
For 85 shows, I walked out, in tribute clear.
Every performance of 'A Bolt From D'Blue' a dedication,
A nod to Malachy's legacy, a celebration.

On his 90th birthday, I wrote a poem to surprise,
A token of gratitude, a moment to recognize.
Sitting in awe in his home with John, Brendan and Fr Pat,
Malachy, a mentor and guide, where memories sat.

In every trip across the pond, in New York's glow,
Malachy's wisdom and friendship continued to grow.
He inspired confidence, gave spotlight when doors closed near,
A beacon in my journey, forever dear.

Rest in peace, Malachy McCourt, your legacy lives on,
A tale of friendship, inspiration, and a bond that's drawn.
As I introduce my poem, a tribute so grand,
For the man who left an indelible mark in this playwright's land.

17

In Cork, where the River Lee winds,
A talent named Cillian Murphy shines.
From Disco Pigs to Shelby's grand schemes,
He conquers Oppenheimer in Oscar dreams.
Irish eyes are smiling for the roles he defines!

18

In dreams, I find myself afloat, adrift at sea,
No course, no plan, just the vastness surrounding me.
On this maiden voyage of peace within,
Confronting demons, a journey to begin.

The sea's breeze, a whisper, a comforting embrace,
As I, a proud Irish playwright, find solace and grace.
Along North County Dublin's coast, I tread,
In the night, to the Irish Sea, my eyes are led.

The voices of my people echo on the waves,
Irish hope and dreams, like dancers in sea caves.
Eyes open, back on shore, demons set free,
By the majestic beauty of the Irish Sea.

In darkness, madness, and love intertwined,
I drift, confront, and let my troubles behind.
The sea, a companion, a canvas of my soul,
With each wave, a step forward, making me whole.

19

In times of darkness, hold on tight,
For lady luck will bring her light.
A sign will come, you'll see it's true,
Life's full of beauty, wonder too.

In shadows deep, where heartaches lie,
There's beauty waiting by and by.
In places where you least expect,
Support and love you will detect.

A friendly call, a listening ear,
A meal shared with those held dear.
A winning bet, a home-cooked meal,
A robin's visit, joy so real.

A candle flickers in the night,
A sunset's glow, pure and bright.
The taste of stout, the kettle's song,
These simple joys, where you belong.

A walk in nature's calm embrace,
Or silent moments in a darkened place.
A book's new chapter, a phone call made,
These acts of hope will never fade.

This poem's for you, a gentle nudge,
That hope exists, it doesn't budge.
In pockets small, in dark and light,
Surprises come to lift your plight.

So thank the stars, the moon, the skies,
For every moment's sweet surprise.
In life's deep valleys, you'll revive,
With every breath, you are alive.

20

I said goodbye,
For the very last time.
When you closed your eyes,
The room went silent,
I felt your soul waltz out the window,
A sadness took complete control of me.

Until one night,
I heard a tap at my window.
The moon illuminated the starless sky,
A soul of stars lit up my heartache.
As I knew your spirit,
From that moment,
Will always be with me.

The memories we shared,
Lifted my senses,
As a gentle reminder.

The music will never die,
Nor the love and our laughter.
As I felt your soul again,
Waltz out the window.

21

You won't be forgotten,
For Ireland calls your name.
Or just another statistic,
On the global stage of life.

But a cherished memory,
For you loved unconditionally.
With a nurturing hand,
And a devilish laugh to boot.

You showed me kindness,
What was wrong and what was right.
You showed me warmth and forgiveness,
Even in your last few days,
On this planet we call life.

I will always light my candles,
For Ireland will never forget your name.
The wind whistles your tune,
The birds sing your ballad.

My life went dark,
Sitting alone in an empty church,
Until a robin flew on my shoulder.

To let me know,
Ireland will always call your name.
Even in the darkest moments,
Your name will always show me light.

22

Brother,
We never found the time to say goodbye,
But that's not how we lived our lives.
There's no manual for grief,
Only time.

Hallowed memories of laughter at the kitchen table,
The ultimate host and drinks companion.
The glass was the measure,
Oh, we soared like kites on countless occasions.

You lived a life without regrets,
Married a lady of poise and grace.
Your energy was infectious,
Your roar still echoes from the side-lines.

Some days are tougher than others,
You were a mountain of a man,
But your presence is always around us.
The bone-crackling sound of a tackle on the pitch,
The clink of glasses toasting family, friendship, or success,

When you beat the odds or the bookie,
Always rockin' a fine tailored suit,
Or a pair of shorts on a winter's day,
You're always here with us.

We drank many a night until the wee hours,
But you always believed in me,
Straight to the point,
Get up and continue the good fight.

Time is a gift we all take for granted,
But your two sons are bold and handsome,
With an army of family and friends behind them,
And a fierce warrior of a mother to lead them.

Brother, we never got to say goodbye,
But that's not how we lived our lives.
Shut up and pour me a drink,
Turn on the music and make it a double,
Or else there'll be trouble.

23

A secret base
We used to hide from the world outside,
When we were just two boys from the Jacko.

Swinging from homemade swings and climbing trees,
Itchy back fights and Mr. Freeze,
Lost in imagination and free to be wild.

A pact was made—
Blood brothers for life
Down by the Valley.

But a darkness took hold of you
That I didn't see.
The dapper man I knew, so full of warmth and banter,
Was swinging alone between the trees.

I miss my blood brother—
Two pints at the bar and the banter.
I cry at night so nobody can see my pain;
I scream by the tracks to drown out my anger.

But this is not a selfish act
Of a man of sane mind,
But a brother so lost—
This was your only answer.

The smell of a joint reminds me of you,
That cheeky glint,
A ladies' man,
Once so full of life.

You're free, my brother—
Free from pain,
Free from darkness.
But why?

When I close my eyes,
I hear our laughter in the trees,
Forever in my mind,
Two best friends,
The boys from the Jacko.

24

It is only when I close my eyes at night,
I see the mistakes I've made throughout my life.
Those crazy days and city nights,
I'm not afraid of dying my friend,
I only fear loneliness and a lack of human touch.

My soul has loved and danced underneath the city glow,
When my head hits the pillow.
I feel like I'm locked down in a penitentiary,
But even on those damp woodland paths grows the wildflower centaury.

For Mother Nature holds my hand,
I take a moment to breathe.
And illuminate my demons from underneath the chemtrails,
Through the power of my dreams.

My imagination saves me from my darkness and demons,
Moments of wild passion overload my senses.
For I am alive,
For I have loved,
For I am free.

About the Publisher

Orla Kelly Publishing is an Irish owned independent publisher based in the suburbs of Cork City. Established by Orla Kelly in 2014, they offer unparalleled support, design and publishing services for their clients. They structure, design, publish, print and undertake online distribution of books cross multiple formats such as ebook, paperback, hardback and audiobooks with all royalties going direct to their clients.

Orla's key specialty is in working with professionals who want to publish high impact-high value strategy books to grow their business or to publish their legacy book where their wisdom and experiences gained over a lifetime are preserved for all time in their book.

Orla's clients gain recognition, credibility, and respect from peers while outshining competitors with their book. From start to finish, they are supported, and provided with the expertise and confidence needed to achieve their publishing dream.

Contact the publisher on getpublished@orlakellypublishing.com or via their website OrlaKellyPublishing.com.

Please Spread the Word

Dear Reader,

Thanks a thousand from the bottom of my heart for purchasing my first book of poetry, 24. Your support means the world to me. If you enjoyed my book, I would be immensely grateful if you could take a moment to leave a review online. Your feedback will help me on my journey and reach more readers who might resonate with my words. Feel free to follow me on social media to stay updated on my latest work and join me in this creative adventure.

Forever a drinker with writing problems,

David

www.ingramcontent.com/pod-product-compliance
Lightning Source LLC
Chambersburg PA
CBHW030312100526
44590CB00012B/612